ECCEI

CONTRAPTIONS

MW01039820

'To invent, you need a good imagination and a pile of junk.'
Thomas Edison

ECCENTRIC
CONTRAPTIONS

and amazing gadgets, gizmos and thingamabobs

MAURICE COLLINS
WITH IAN KEAREY

David & Charles

To my grandchildren, Nicky and Emma
MC

A DAVID & CHARLES BOOK

First published in the UK in 2004

Copyright © Maurice Collins 2004

Distributed in North America
by F&W Publications, Inc.
4700 East Galbraith Road
Cincinnati, OH 45236
1-800-289-0963

Maurice Collins has asserted his right to be identified as author of this
work in accordance with the Copyright, Designs and Patents Act, 1988.

All rights reserved. No part of this publication may be reproduced, stored in a
retrieval system, or transmitted, in any form or by any means, electronic or
mechanical, by photocopying, recording or otherwise, without prior permission
in writing from the publisher.

A catalogue record for this book is available from the British Library.

ISBN 0 7153 1822 5 hardback
ISBN 0 7153 1821 7 paperback

Printed in Singapore by KHL Printing Co Pte Ltd
for David & Charles
Brunel House   Newton Abbot   Devon

Commissioning Editor Neil Baber
Desk Editor Lewis Birchon
Executive Art Editor Ali Myer
Designer Jodie Lystor
Production Controller Jennifer Campbell

Visit our website at www.davidandcharles.co.uk

David & Charles books are available from all good bookshops; alternatively you can
contact our Orderline on (0)1626 334555 or write to us at FREEPOST EX2110,
David & Charles Direct, Newton Abbot, TQ12 4ZZ (no stamp required UK mainland).

Contents

Preface

It all started down a five-foot trench in an old rubbish dump in Sittingbourne in Kent. My son Paul, then aged 12, pulled from the side wall of the 'dig' a pointed bottle that had an embossed surface. We both looked at this peculiar container, unable to fathom its use. A few minutes later, another embossed bottle emerged, this time with a marble in its neck – and that was the beginning of my interest in everyday, labour-saving and plain weird contraptions from the past.

I did some research, and found that in the early 1800s fizzy drinks manufacturers had a problem stopping gas escaping from their products. In 1814, in a patent application for a bottle-filling machine, William Hamilton sketched a bottle with a pointed bottom that had to lie on its side, ensuring that the cork always remained wet and didn't shrink, allowing the gas to escape. This remained the common method of bottling until 1875, when Hiram Codd patented the marble stopper, which had to be hit into a recess in the bottle to allow the contents to be poured or drunk – hence the phrase 'a load of codswallop'. So the mystery of the bottles in the wall was solved.

Thus began a 30-year passion for finding quirky, everyday gadgets used by people in the past; the more eccentric and unusual the better; the more effort for less reward the more satisfying; the more ingenuity used to solve the simplest problems – often in the hope of making a fortune – the more exciting. The resulting collection can be categorized by use, by period of patent, by the energy that drives the mechanisms, or even by the way they look, but the key to my interest in each whatchamacallit was the quirkiness of its use in everyday life. If it was intended to save labour and make life easier for the user – and even better, if it didn't succeed – then it met my criteria.

For this book the objects have been grouped in categories loosely termed domestic, the kitchen, business (or commercial), social (or personal), medical and transport, along with a few miscellaneous items that don't fit any of these but which demanded inclusion. There are over 400 items in my collection, of which the book shows just a sample, but there are probably thousands of weird gadgets still out there. Don't throw them away – there will be someone just around the corner waiting to see them and put them on show so that everyone can enjoy the ingenuity of the human race in its unceasing search for a problem-free life.

Although the gadgets themselves are somewhat past any useful application, in many cases the principles are sound. In fact, I have used the gadgets to great effect helping young entrepreneurs to brainstorm new products and potential business ideas.

Of course, a great part of the fascination of these gizmos is trying to work out what they are for when you see them for the first time. Why not test your powers of knowledge and intuition by placing your hand over the text on each left-hand page while you look at the image on the right? Have fun – and no peeking!

Maurice Collins

Domestic

'Household tasks are easier and quicker when they are done by somebody else.'
James Thorpe

Teasmade

The Victorians and Edwardians were
mad keen on their morning cup of tea,
and would go to ingenious lengths to
make it without having to get out of
bed. This beautiful brass and copper
teamaker was patented in 1902 in
Birmingham. When the alarm clock
triggered the switch, a match was struck,
lighting a spirit stove under the kettle.
When the water came to the boil, the
steam pressure lifted a hinged flap,
allowing the kettle to tilt and fill the
teapot; then a plate swung over the
stove and extinguished the flames.

Automatic shaver

The 1930s saw an explosion of clever
devices made of Bakelite, Leo Baekeland's
revolutionary material; this is one of the
oddest. The little brush at the end of the
line is not just for cleaning the shaver's
blades – you also have to pull it firmly
to get the blades rotating. You then apply
the shaver to the face and hope to shave
an area before the blades slow down,
thereby trapping the bristles and ripping
off your skin. Did we say 'clever'?

Burglar alarm

This clockwork burglar alarm dates from the 1870s. The mechanism was wound up and the upright was set, then the alarm was placed at the foot of a door with the spike pushed into the carpet or a floorboard. If anyone attempted to open the door, the upright would be pushed down and set off the bell. It's quite loud and effective.

Knot unpicker

With keen Boy Scouts loose around the house, the knot unpicker would have been a boon and a blessing to any harassed mother in the 1920s.

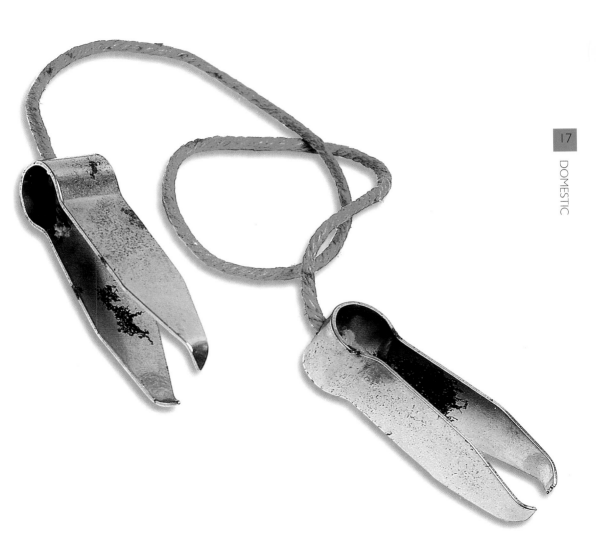

Salesman's washing machine

Complete with mangle, this 1894 washing
machine works on the same principles as
today's machines, agitating the clothes in
a drum. This example has survived partly
because it was not worn out in a busy
household: it is a small-scale model used
by an American salesman. He would
transport the sample machine from shop
to shop, giving demonstrations at each
stop and taking orders for the real thing.

Two-iron heater

This efficient German machine from the beginning of the 20th century heats two flat irons by gas; when one is ready for use, the machine swivels to heat the other. You could probably fabricate such a heater today – but wouldn't it look dull compared with this magnificent example of the metalworker's art and soaring Biedermeier imagination?

Pin dispenser

*'See a pin and pick it up, and all day
long you'll have...a pin.'*

This mid-1920s pin dispenser aimed to
replace the boring old pincushion with
an up-to-date alternative. Remove the
top and fill the base with pins – with
the heads up, remember! – replace the
top and press it to deliver a shiny new
pin each time. Pincushions are available
to this day.

Go-to-bed vestas

This early 1900s French device solved
the problem of lighting a candle at night –
the candle was the match was the candle.
It was ignited by striking the wick against
an abrasive strip at one end of the box,
and was then stuck upright in the holder
to give illumination. The charming picture
on the box makes it worth the effort.

Clockwork fire blower

Hallowed by age they might be, but the time-honoured methods of igniting a fire using bellows or with a lot of blowing and swearing didn't cut a lot of ice with one late-Victorian mastermind. Wind the handle of the fire blower, hook the front part to the front of the grate and direct the nozzle into the fire – and you could probably cover the room with soot and ashes in five seconds flat.

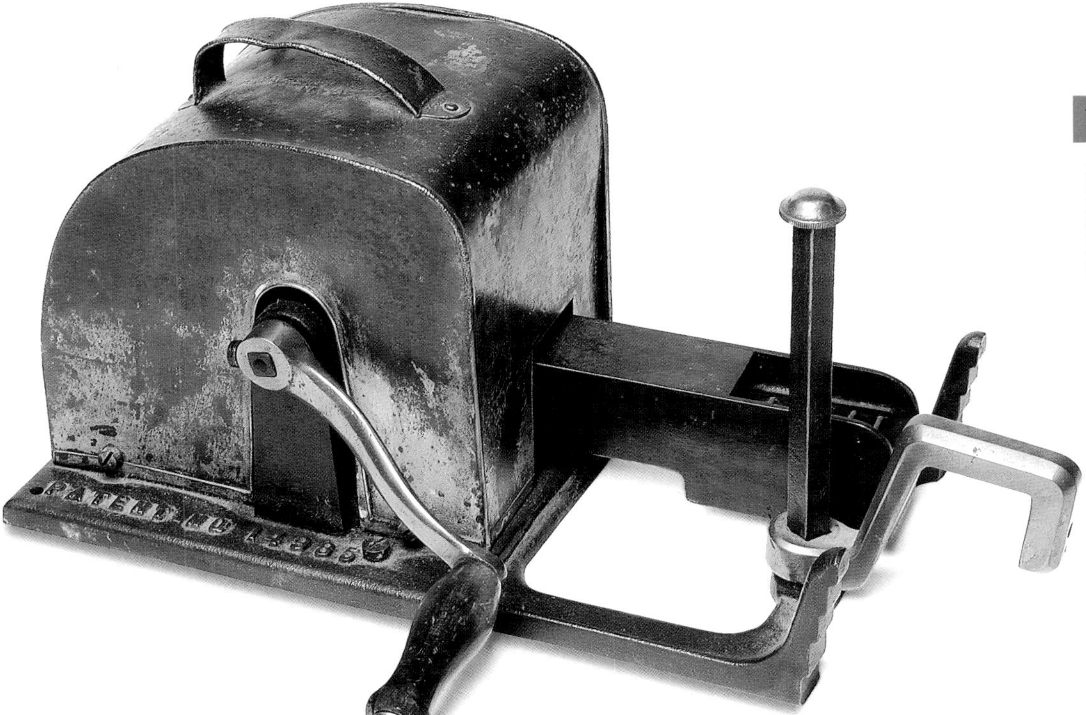
PATENT

Ruff iron

This little ruff iron from the 1880s is
a simple solution to a potentially time-
consuming problem: the lower part is
heated over a fire, the collar or sleeve
is placed over it and the roller is pressed
along it to make perfect ruffs. Versions
of this iron are still in use among Amish
communities in the USA.

Wind-up lamp

Glass lamp funnels didn't last long in the
trenches of World War I, so this ingenious
oil lamp avoided the need to use glass at
all. The clockwork mechanism at the base
was wound up, and as it unwound it
fanned a slow and gentle breeze through
the lamp onto the wick, keeping the flame
alight. It was still a bad move to try to light
three cigarettes off it, however.

Shade remover

Glass shades were obviously as liable to
break as electric light bulbs in Victorian
days, but the 'Facile' shade remover
made the task of replacing them, well,
facile. Look at the illustration on the
instructions: if there were any broken
pieces of glass, wouldn't they fall straight
down the user's sleeve?

The "Facile" Electric Shade Remover

HARRISON'S PATENT

INCANDESCENT LAMPS.
CAUTION.
One Lamp looks the same as another

You should however be warned against purchasing a cheap lamp which in appearance is often the same as the more expensive. By doing this you run a certain risk of considerably increasing your electricity account, besides the annoyance of lamps continually breaking and a decided falling ... being in...

ELECTRIC SHADE

NO MORE BROKEN SHADES

QUICK AND SAFE

The "Facile" Electric Shade Remover

... ALWAYS USED

EASILY APPLIED.

DIRECTIONS FOR USE

Toilet chain air freshener

Before the days of aerosols, this refillable
device emitted a puff of Phul-Nana or
some other popular mid-1920s perfume
each time the chain on the high-level
cistern was pulled. The atmosphere in
the smallest room must have been
intense on party nights.

Iron/kettle

So long as there was an electricity supply
nearby, using the two-in-one portable iron
and kettle the intrepid traveller of the
1920s could be sure of hot water for
that essential cup of tea while pressing
his or her clothes.

Cotton reel tidy

Wartime rationing in the UK didn't end suddenly with victory in 1945: there were shortages of just about everything, and a plethora of useful devices to save materials appeared on the market. Using a cotton reel tidy, there was no waste of precious thread for mending the demob suit or the best pre-war frock.

IMPROVED

Cotton Reel Tidy

100 YARDS.

HOLD LIKE THIS
and get a free
running thread.

7 for 6d.

NO UNTIDY ENDS
OR DIRTY COTTON.

YOU PULL WHAT
YOU NEED & LEAVE
REMAINDER TIGHT.

JUST CLIP ON AND
SLIDE COTTON
THROUGH SLOT.

Knitting ball holder

When you see the illustration on the box, the use of this Edwardian device becomes clear. However, to the casual observer it looks like a particularly unpleasant medieval torture device.

THE
ST. GEORGE

Pat. Applied
For.

Regd.

KNITTING BALL HOLDER.

Vacuum cleaner

1907's answer to the Dyson, the 'Entirely
British' Baby Daisy (even the name is
redolent of a different era) was at the
cutting edge of vacuum cleaner design.
No matter that you had to pump the
bellows briskly while moving the miniscule
head across the floor, it was still the best
friend of many a housewife and maid.

Fire alarm

There will always be a need for fire
protection and alarms, and it has inspired
the invention of all sorts of contraptions.
In this 1910 example, the principle was
that as the plastic holder melted in the
heat, it would allow the claw circle to
drop, make an electrical connection
and set off the alarm.

Curfew guard

This was placed in front of a fire at the
end of the day to prevent stray sparks
setting fire to the carpet. With its expanse
of curved brass (to be polished every
day) and fine late-Victorian handle, it
looks like a cross between a breastplate
and an old fireman's helmet.

The Kitchen

'There has always been a food processor in the kitchen. But once upon a time she was usually called the missus or Mom.'
Sue Berkman

Doughnut filler

Bicycle pump? Never! Syringe? Pah! The only way to fill a doughnut with jam is to force it in with one push of the lever of this 1930s doughnut filler. However, it's reassuring to know that it doesn't take specialist equipment – just an injudicious bite – to give the jam its freedom once more, usually all over your clothes.

Whistling kettle

If it wasn't in this book and made out of copper, you would swear that Blood's patent whistling kettle of around 1875 – the first such noisy kitchen implement – with its pure, minimalist lines, was a clever, possibly Scandinavian, modern design: *'Plus ça change, plus c'est la même chose.'*

Nursery food warmer

In Victorian houses, where the nursery
might be some considerable distance from
the kitchen, food and drinks for infants and
invalids could be warmed up on the spot
by placing a candle in the base of this
pyramid food warmer.

Two-cherry pipper

'I gave my love two cherries…'

The cherries were placed in the hopper
and the twin spikes were plunged into a
pair of fruits, which were then pushed off
the spikes automatically, minus their
stones. This simple late-Victorian device
really does speed up what can otherwise
be a tedious process.

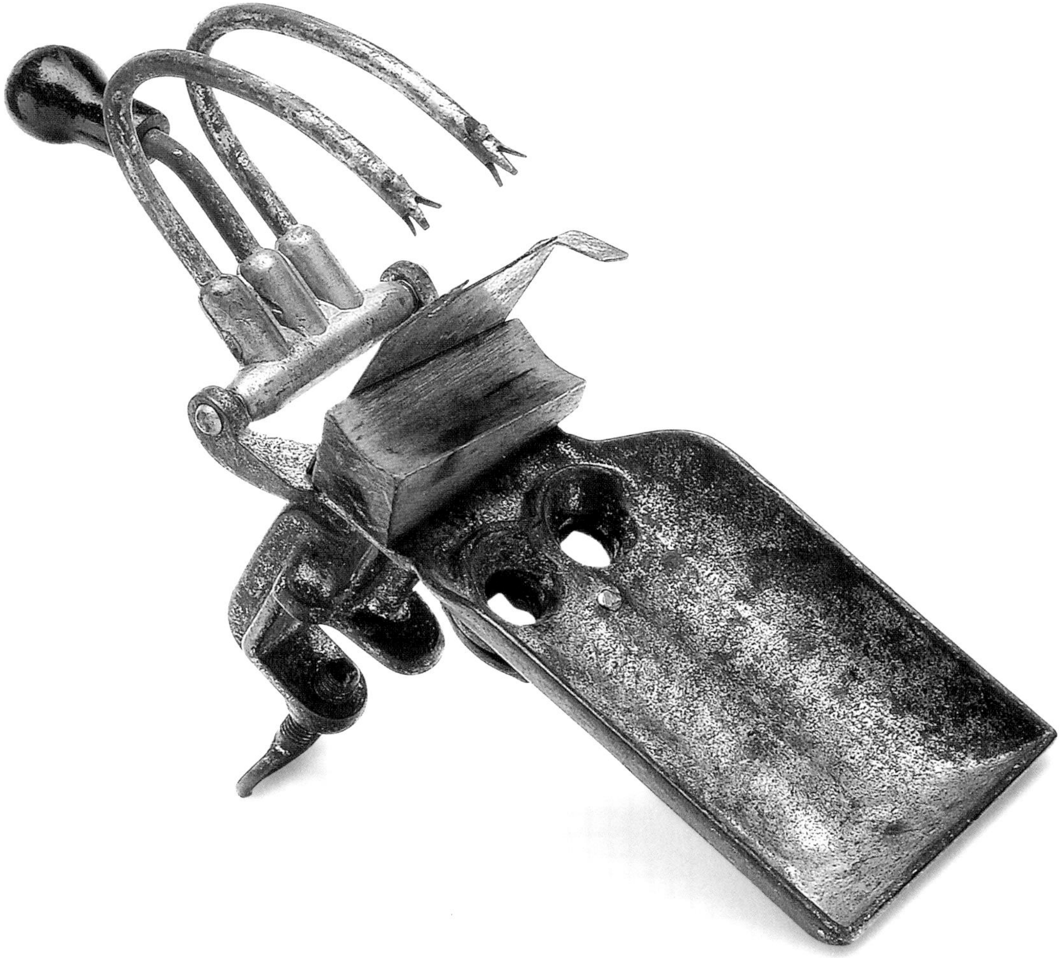

Bottle washer

Anyone who washes bottles for reuse or recycling knows that some are difficult to clean thoroughly. When the handle of this 1920s French bottle washer is turned, water is pumped into the bottle and the wires spin outwards.

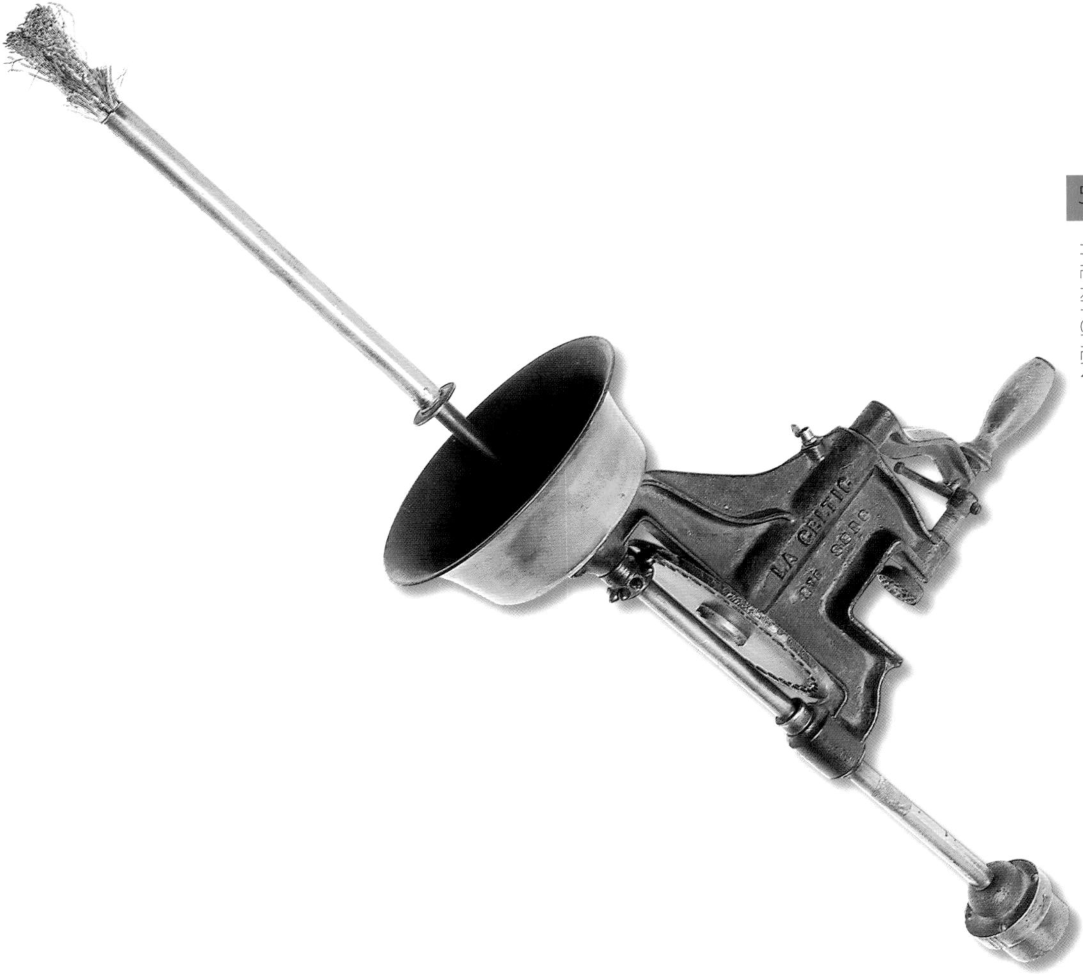
LA CELTIC

Food processor

Mr Kent, the London maker of this splendid late-Victorian multi-purpose food preparer, described himself as 'Patentee of Inventions Promoting Domestic Economy'. It sliced, ground, grated and shredded, all in one compact package, just like the gadgets advertised today, but with the advantage of using no greater power source than turning the handle.

Circular knife sharpener

This circular knife sharpener is an
interesting Edwardian variation on the
more standard types, and was intended
for large households that used a great
deal of cutlery at every meal. Knife
powder was placed inside the machine,
the knives were positioned with the
blades inside the outer leather casing,
then the handle was turned.

Peach peeler

If you really need to peel a peach – which
seems a singularly pointless occupation –
this 1870s peach peeler is a must. To the
uninitiated, the machine looks like nothing
so much as one of the many patent apple
peelers invented around the same time,
but it was designed for peaches and
peaches only, and had to be kept and
used separately.

Hand grape press

It would take an awfully long time to press
enough grapes for a vat of wine, but this
little domestic press from the late 19th
century was useful for making grape juice
or wine for the family.

Soda bottles

Lying down is the Hamilton bottle, with
the pointed base and flat side, mentioned
in the Preface. It ruled the roost for over
60 years. Standing up is an example of the
Codd bottle patented in 1875, complete
with marble stopper and recess in the
neck. Early Codd bottles had the same
pointed base as Hamilton's, until it was
realized that more could be stacked in
a case by standing them upright.

Wind-up timer

This is what clockwork kitchen timers
looked like in the mid-1890s, before they
began to impersonate tomatoes, onions,
eggs, Snoopys, doughnuts, burgers, golf
balls, footballs, Bart Simpsons, bagels, etc.

Sausage maker

It may look as though it should be in
the Medical or Transport sections of this
book, but this is a domestic sausage maker
from the early 1900s. Sausage meat was
placed in the tin container, the skin was
pushed over the funnel, and the wooden
rammer forced the meat into the skin,
producing perfect custom-made bangers
every time.

Food chopper

Using a modern food processor is easy –
fill the machine and push the switch.
How much more satisfying to use this
late-Victorian food chopper: turning the
handle pushes the chopping arm forcefully
up and down, while rotating the bowl at
the same time.

Raisin cleaner

This machine was used in grocery shops
at the end of the 19th century. When
sacks of raisins or currants were delivered,
they were opened and the contents were
poured into the chute. The machine then
sorted the fruit from the chaff and other
assorted rubbish, often sifting everything
twice – through a coarse and then a fine
sifting attachment.

Pea podder

So far, this is the only example of this
machine that we have come across. The
instructions on the side are very hard to
decipher, but it is thought to date from
around 1890. The action is simple: put
the pea pods into the hopper, turn the
handle and the fresh peas emerge from
the side, with the pods extruded
separately as waste.

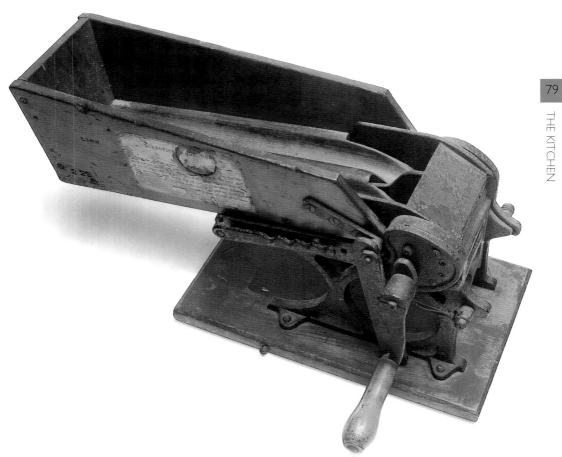

Washing machine

Banish those washday blues with this
wonderful wooden washing machine. It
dates from around 1900, although similar
designs had already been around for half
a century. The principle should be familiar:
put the clothes into the tub, which has a
ribbed interior, add water and soap, then
close the lid and turn the handle as fast as
you can. Empty the machine and use the
mangle to squeeze the water out of the
clothes. Cleanliness and fitness in one go!

Emulsifier

A posh name for a highly geared whisk
in a large ceramic bowl, the emulsifier was
used to mix food in the kitchens of stately
homes in late-Victorian days.

 # Business

'Technological progress has merely provided us with more efficient means for going backwards.'
Aldous Huxley

Label gummer

Using the late-Victorian wonder fluid,
Gumolene, and a series of rollers, the
'Indispensable' gumming machine promised
to gum labels, paper and envelopes with
just a turn of the handle.

Envelope sealer

This splendid machine by Reynolds of
Chicago dates from the late 19th century,
when gravitas and efficiency ruled the day
and it was every businessman's ambition to
be able to fill the office with labour-saving
whatnots like this. As you crank the lever a
roller drives the open envelope through a
wetting process, then another roller finally
seals the envelope.

Calculator

Now that most things numerical can be
done by activating a microchip, another
lost art is that of using a manual calculator
efficiently. The Sun adding machine dates
from 1902, and was brought into action
by using the metal stylus to flick and move
each row of figures; a skilled operator was
an asset to any business.

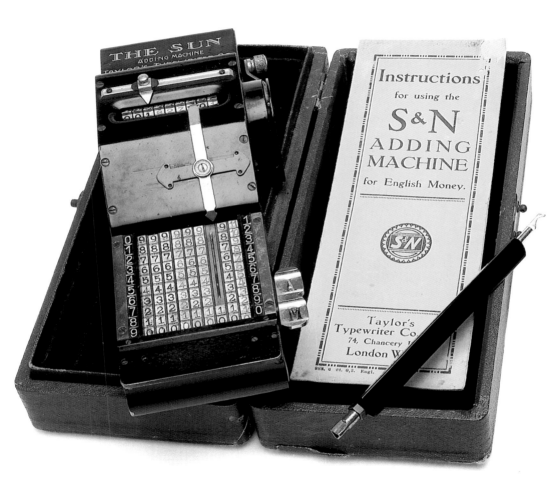

Cheque stamper

An almost forgotten method of preventing
cheque fraud was embossing the amount
on the cheque, rather than writing it –
it was well-nigh impossible to alter the
figures without the change being detected.
This American cheque stamper was made
at the beginning of the 20th century.

Office time stamp

In the days when London businesses could count on at least four or five postal deliveries per day (*and* not have to pay extra for the privilege), receiving the mail was a pretty full-time occupation. It wasn't enough just to log the day the post was received – you also needed to know what time it arrived. This precision time stamp dates from about 1900.

'Gatling' stapler

Most of us don't see office machines as
exciting – functional, yes, but lacking that
something extra that makes the world
sit up and take notice. King, a London
manufacturer in Victorian times, tried
to beef up his undoubtedly stalwart
stapler by calling it the 'Gatling', thereby
borrowing some reflected glory from the
slightly more famous gun invented by the
American RJ Gatling. It looks more like a
scorpion than a gun.

Pawnbroker's pledge maker

If you were unlucky enough to have
to visit Uncle's and pop your weasel, this
mahogany and brass desk would show
you that your Victorian pawnbroker was
a man of means. The whole mechanism,
by which an original pawn ticket and up
to three copies could be written out
simultaneously, is finely balanced and
swings away when not in use.

Gold coin changer

Lord Peter Wimsey, the detective hero
of the books by Dorothy L Sayers, used
to carry six gold sovereigns at all times
because it made him feel good (what
it did to the line of his trousers is not
mentioned). In the real world of the
late 19th century, however, few cabmen
and other such minions would have had
change for such a grand sum as a pound,
so machines like this were installed in
gentlemen's clubs to supply change.

Change machine

Apart from its florid cast-metal curlicues –
as if they weren't enough – the Brandt
Junior machine from the 1920s is
remarkable for its keys: they offer a
great variety of now-forgotten sums
to ring up – 8/6d, 3/7d, farthings or
halfpennies, anyone?

Firkin barrel

Dating from the late-Victorian era, this is a mini firkin or cider barrel. While the master would have a full-sized one to carry to work, the apprentice would attach this eight-inch version to his belt or shoulder strap.

Social

'You can discover more about a person in an hour of play than in a year of conversation.'
Plato

Double cigarette holder

They knew how to enjoy themselves in
the 1920s: this double cigarette holder
could take two high-tar, unfiltered gaspers
at once. It may have been inspired by
the cigarette case belonging to Bulldog
Drummond, hero of Sapper's bestselling
crime novels of the day; it held 'Turkish
one side, Virginian the other.'

Toe protectors

Marketed as being able to cut hosiery bills
by up to 80 per cent during World War II,
these sock protectors were intended to
be worn on the big toes. Clipping one's
toenails regularly could have produced
the same effect.

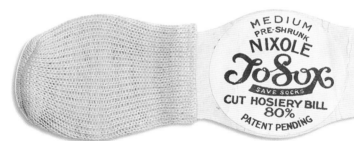

Page turner

These days, a 'page turner' is a novel
you can't put down, but here the term
describes this gadget dating from 1905,
designed to help musicians. You can set
up a few pages ready to be turned by
inserting the top of each metal rod into
the page and setting it to be held. Pull
the catch free, and the page flips over.

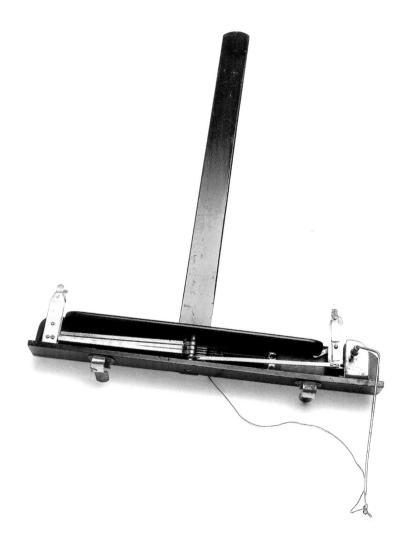

Honour box

This'll test your honesty: insert a coin
in the slot to open the lid, then help
yourself to the right amount of tobacco
or snuff and close the late-Victorian box
again. Stalin is reputed to have had one
of these boxes made, operated by a timer
instead of a coin, to help him cut down
his smoking. However, he then forced
the maker to tell him, under threat of
an unpleasant and protracted death, how
to cheat and open the box whenever he
needed a snout – which says a lot about
his sense of honour.

Hat measurer

Where would Victorian comic fiction and
cartoons, or Charlie Chaplin and Laurel
and Hardy, come to that, have been
without people putting on hats of the
wrong size with wearisome regularity?
Anyone with any money (and often those
without) would have their head measured
for a custom-made hat by a machine such
as this. It's extremely heavy, so you'd hope
your hatter was a fast worker.

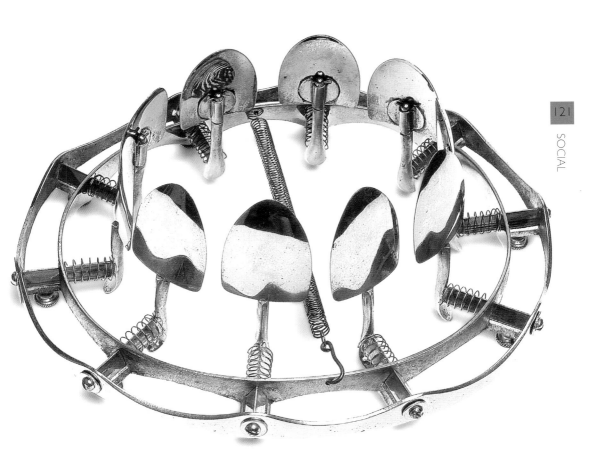

Miser's purse

Versions of these leather purses have been around for centuries – Horatio Nelson used one – but very few have survived; this one is Victorian. You put your money into the opening in the middle, pulled the two large metal washers into position to ensure that the money in the ends could not be reached, then wore the purse over your belt. Impulse buys were obviously not the order of the day.

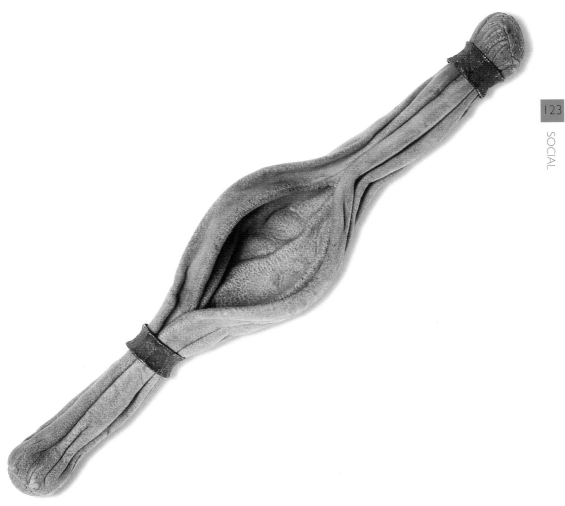

Linen damp tester

In these days of overheated and air-conditioned hotel rooms, the threat of inadequately dried bedlinen has been largely forgotten, but it was a real health hazard for previous generations. The proprietors of a Folkestone hotel in the 1920s gave these damp testers to guests, gaining customer loyalty – everybody likes a free gift – and at the same time casting aspersions on the condition of their competitors' sheets. Clever.

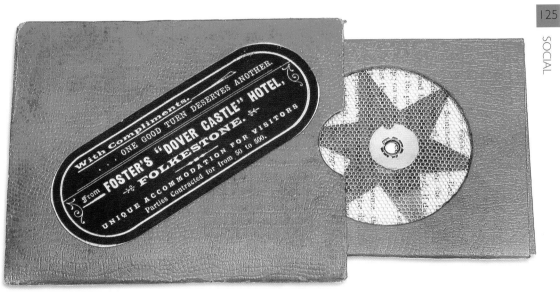

With Compliments,

. . ONE GOOD TURN DESERVES ANOTHER.

FOSTER'S "DOVER CASTLE" HOTEL,

from FOLKESTONE.

UNIQUE ACCOMMODATION FOR VISITORS

Parties Contracted for from 50 to 500.

Watch the birdie

Photographers still say 'Watch the birdie', and here is the item that inspired the phrase. Water was poured into the bottom compartment and a rubber tube was then attached to the pipe in the middle. The bird would be placed on top of the large plate camera, the photographer would blow through the tube, the bird would trill, the child subject would smile and the shot would be taken. Or so the theory went. Why, then, do most Victorian children still look solemn or downright miserable in photographs?

Money box clock

When cash was tight for many people
after World War II, landlords, insurance
companies and others all tried to ensure
that what little money there was went to
them first. One insurance company gave
away this money box clock; a florin (10
pence) was dropped into the slot at
intervals, keeping the clock running until
the tallyman came and collected the
money at the end of the week.

SOCIAL

129

Hand-operated fan

To keep cool in the hot summers of
the 1930s, a Bakelite fan was just the
ticket. Generated by pumping the lever
with your finger, it was also jolly useful,
given that batteries were definitely not
included in those days.

Moustache protectors

From Victorian days well into the 20th
century, getting the mulligatawny onto
your moustache at dinner could set you
down as a bounder or a cad at the very
least. A moustache protector spoon or
cup would save the day. It was, of course,
too much to expect you to carry your
own cutlery and crockery when invited
out, so you took the little attachment for
a cup or glass instead.

Lying down spectacles

When you're too tired to raise your
head but still want to catch up on some
uplifting and moral reading (Ruskin always
sends us to sleep), these late-Victorian
spectacles with mirrors attached would
enable you to rest the book on your
chest, rather than getting arm-ache
from holding the volume above you.
A headboard and a couple of extra
pillows would do the trick, too.

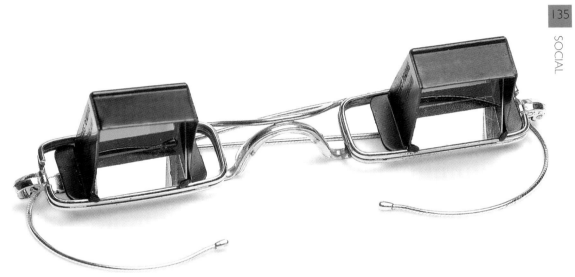

Pistol purse

'Stand back – I have a gun and I'm not afraid to use it!'

To protect one's honour, property and even life, this 1884 pistol purse cunningly concealed the dainty weapon in one side. The gun carried one small bullet only, so the owner had to make the shot count.

Skirt lifter

While horse-drawn transport and
unmetalled roads ruled, the long skirts
worn by ladies put them at a serious
disadvantage in terms of keeping their
garments clean. This is an elegant example
of a skirt lifter from 1879: the metal pads
were fixed to the bottom of the skirt, the
loop of ribbon was draped over the arm,
and the skirt was lifted by raising the arm.
It was also useful for going up and down
stairs without tripping over the skirt.

Travelling candle shade

When travelling in the 1850s, you took
what lighting you could get in inns and
hotels. This portable candle shade was
the forerunner of the dimmer switch
and was used to soften or diffuse the
light; it is beautifully made, and can be
folded to fit into a tiny case no bigger
than a matchbox.

Wig iron

For that fresh-as-a-daisy look in court,
a Victorian lawyer or judge would spend
a few happy minutes in the chambers
beforehand, freshening the curls in his wig
with his wig iron. Rumours that it was also
heated up and applied to tender portions
of the accused's anatomy, to obtain a plea
of guilty, are completely unfounded.

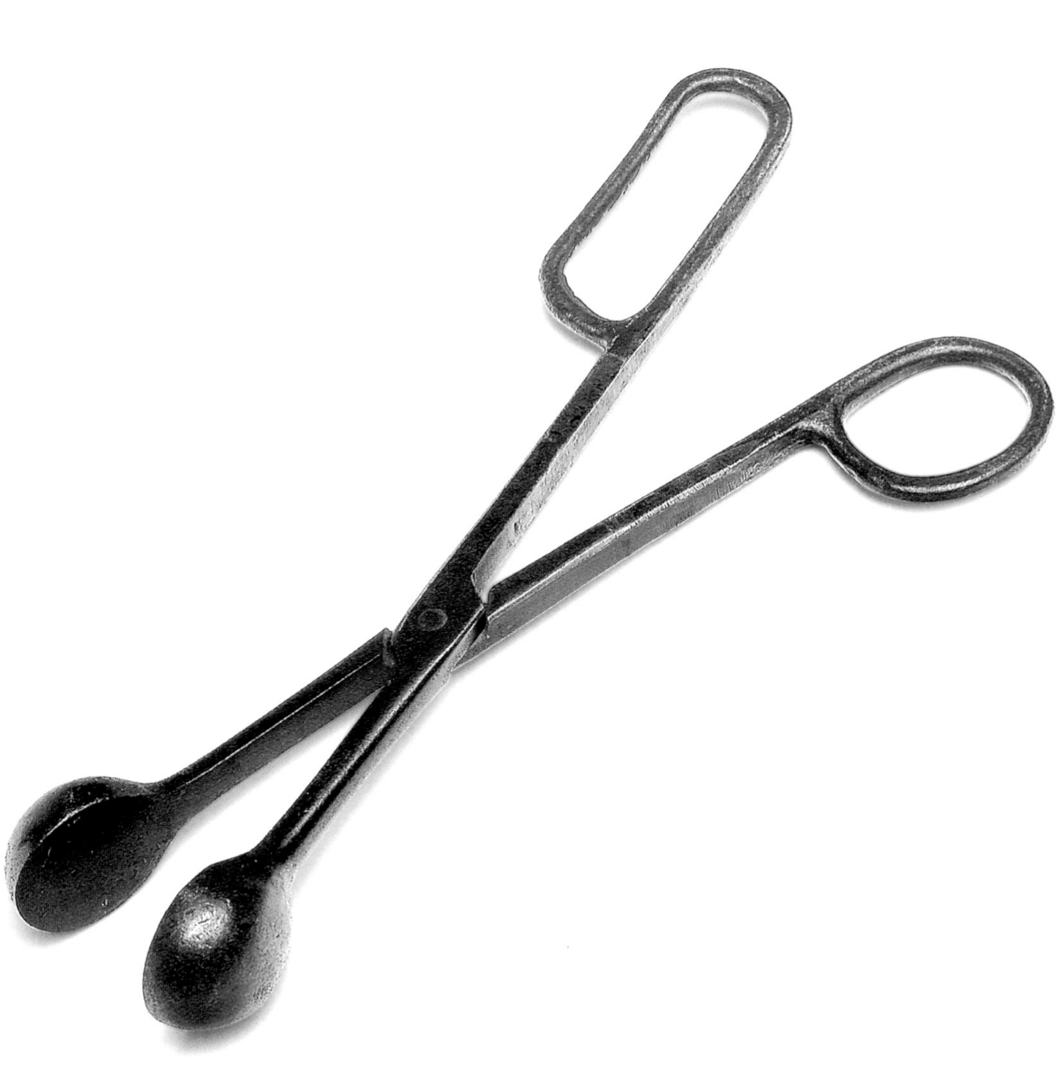

Luggage holder

As you walk up the gangplank of the
RMS *Berengaria*, ready for that luxurious
cruise across the Atlantic, the handle of
your suitcase breaks. Never fear: you
always carry one of these versatile
luggage holders with you for just such
an eventuality, and it is the work of a
minute to fasten the device in place
and continue your progress. No wonder
people look back at the 1920s with a
sense of nostalgia.

Champagne fountain starter

The tradition of building a mountain
of champagne glasses and then trying to
fill as many as possible from one bottle
(or more) is an old one – but it took the
thrifty Victorians to devise a way to avoid
wasting the precious bubbly. This was
placed at the very top of the pyramid,
and the holes in the base distributed the
champagne equally over the glasses below.

Lock key protector

Thefts from hotel rooms were as much a
problem in the 1920s as they are today, so
this lock key protector was a very useful
device. The thick end was inserted into
the lock and the thin barrel was turned,
leaving the thick part in place to prevent
any key, even a skeleton one, being tried.

Ring cigarette holder

The sophisticated Edwardian smoker
would place the ring of this cigarette
holder on a finger and then place a
cigarette in the holder part. What
happened if he forgot about the lighted
end and scratched his head or consulted
his wristwatch is not recorded.

Player harmonica

On the face of it, the Rolmonica, from
the 1920s, was a logical development
of the player piano or pianola: a roll of
perforated paper was fed through the
machine and the notes would play when
air passed through the holes, impressing
bystanders with the user's apparent
musical ability. One small problem – how
would the hapless and unmusical user
know when to blow or suck?

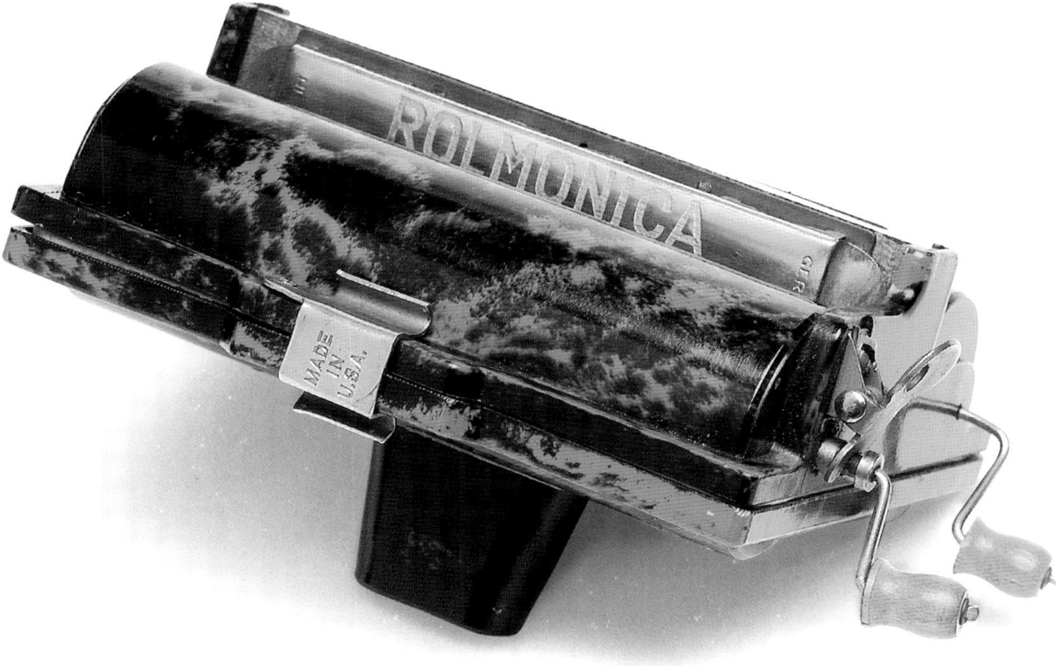
ROLMONICA
MADE
IN
U.S.A.

Tie guide

Oh, the decisions facing the well-dressed
Victorian gentleman as he contemplated
his wardrobe each morning: would he
have his natty neckwear in a Windsor
knot, a four-in-hand, a Prince of Wales
knot or one of the numerous other
variations of the time? Whichever he
chose, his clever tie guide ensured he'd
step out looking neat around the collar.

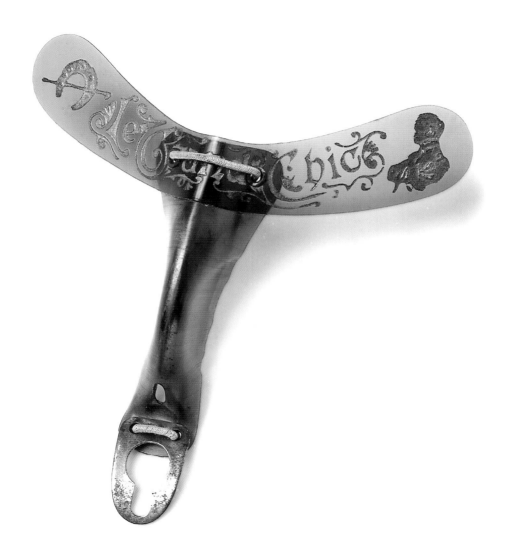

Cap lighter

The Edwardian Papa may have confiscated
little Tommy's cap gun, not because the
dear little chap was making too much
noise, but because Papa needed the
caps to refill his cap cigar lighter. The
hammer strikes a cap to ignite the
wick, obviously with a satisfying bang.

Tobacco plug cutter

Here's handy – just place your plug of
chewing tobacco on the wooden plank,
set the size and turn the handle, and the
cutter will do all the work. What has
happened to these machines in the 80
or so years since they were made; do you
know anyone who still cuts plugs of baccy?

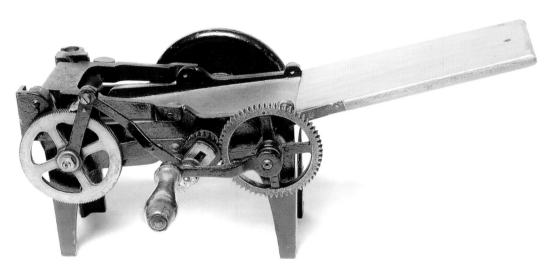

Mutoscope

'What the Butler Saw' was a staple of
piers and amusement arcades for most
of the 20th century, featuring everything
from 'naughty' and risqué shows, like the
one here, to two-minute comedies and
dramas. At one time, before films took
over, the largest arcade in New York had
over a thousand Mutoscopes under one
roof, all with photos flicking away merrily
on their hand-cranked reels.

Moustache trimmer

Rather like an old hedge trimmer, this
fearsome-looking early-20th-century
moustache neatener works by pressing
the spring-loaded handle so that the blade
runs across the trimmer to cut the hairs.
The results were about as accurate as
using an old hedge trimmer, too.

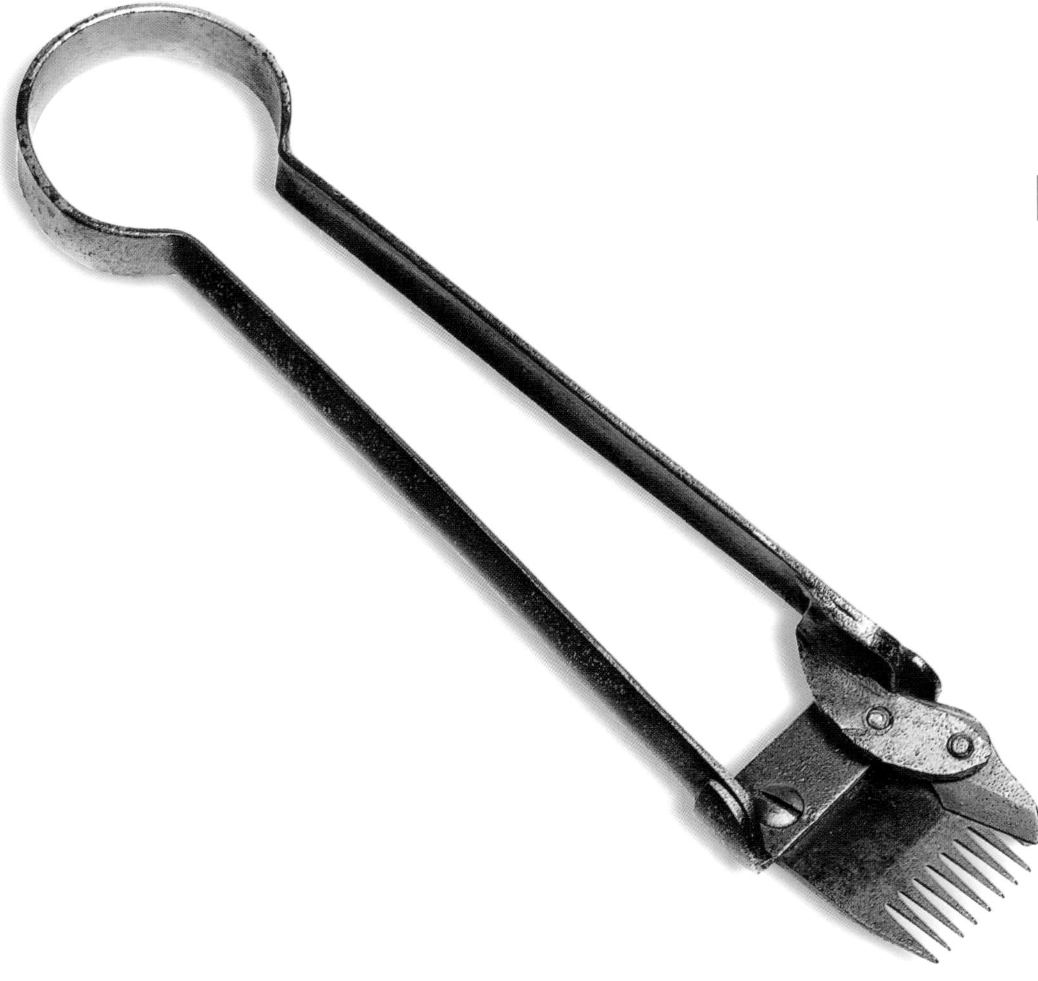

Mini stereoscope

The stereoscope – whereby the eyes,
looking at two flat photographs, see one
3D image – was a massively popular
mid-Victorian invention that spawned
a number of variants. One was this tiny
version, which folds up into a pretty gilt
case and has everything the big type has.

# Medical

'The art of medicine consists in amusing the patient while nature cures the disease.'
Voltaire

Laurance staminator

'Physical perfection within the reach of all',
eh? It's amazing what you can do with a
couple of 1930s bungees, a wallpaper
roller or two, an elastic school belt, Dad's
old pair of braces and a lot of chutzpah.

Ear flatteners

Sadly – or perhaps not so sadly – only
the box remains of this 19th-century
American aid to physical perfection;
the contents must have been used to
destruction. The ear flatteners might have
been worn with comfort, but we doubt
without embarrassment.

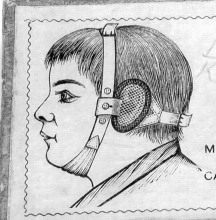

FRED. HASLAM & CC.,

APPARATUS

TO PREVENT PROJECTING EARS.

MADE IN TWO SIZES, PRICE $1.50 EACH

CAN BE WORN WITH COMFORT DURING SLEEP

Dynamo massager

The great days of the quack mountebank
with his universal cure-all may have
gone, but the urge to discover a single,
all-encompassing panacea is as strong as
ever. This 1930s dynamo massager gave
little electric shocks wherever it was
applied; they might not cure you, but they
certainly let you know you were still alive.

ELEKTROLLER

for HEALTH, BEAUTY, SUPPLENESS, STRENGTH.

Ointment applicator

With some medical contraptions, you just *know* that the inventor never suffered from the ailment the device was intended to alleviate or cure. Ointment was placed inside the wooden shaft of this applicator, the blunt end was inserted into the appropriate orifice and then the screw was turned (a difficult task on your own, to say the least – did you phone a friend for help?) until the soothing ointment came out of the holes. We'd rather suffer the complaint, thank you.

'Cure-all' medical electric belt

The discovery of electricity and the
mystery that surrounded how it worked,
created an industry devoted to promoting
this energy as a solution to all the ills
known to mankind. The batteries, held in
small pockets stitched into the belt, were
recharged with a mixture of cider vinegar
and water. Items similar to this late-19th-
century device were made and sold right
up to the mid-20th century.

MEDICAL

Allgemeine Gebrauchsanweisungen

für

Dr. Horne's Elektrische Gürtel.

Der Gürtel wird vor dem Versande genau geprüft und muss richtig funktioniren solls nach Vorschrift behandelt. Nach Empfang des

DIRECTIONS FOR USING DR. HORNE'S ELECTRIC BELT.

The Belt, when you receive it, is arranged just as it should be worn. Examine it carefully, noting how it is put together and where the attachments are connected.

When you wish to use the Belt, remove the chain battery from the cloth case by unhooking the hooks from the rings at each end and drawing the chain or battery out of the case. Then roll the battery up and place it on end in a cup of any kind containing about one-half cider vinegar (common cooking vinegar will do), and one-half water, sufficient to cover the chain or battery. The first time you charge battery let it stay in solution fifteen minutes; after that only two to five minutes.

Then remove the battery from the solution and wipe it with a ragor towel. Place the two ends of the battery to the tip of your tongue lightly

Wafer pill papers

*'A spoonful of sugar helps the medicine
go down…'*
In the early 1900s the most you could
hope for was a wafer of rice paper
wrapped around a nasty-tasting pill: by
the time the wafer dissolved, the pill
was hopefully well past the point where
it could be tasted.

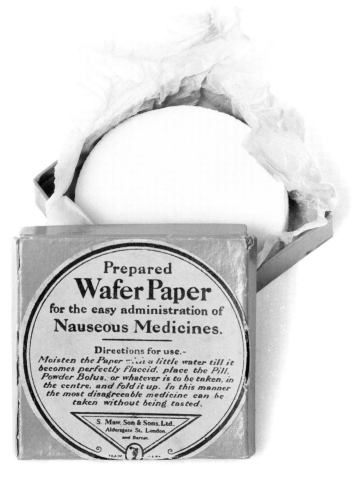

Eye massager

After a day spent travelling in polluted city streets and sitting glued to millions of pixels on a computer screen, what better rest cure for tired eyes could there be than this 1920s eye massager? Well, an eye bath, no television and an early night seems preferable to placing this gadget to the face and pressing the rubber bellows to puff the massaging air onto the eyes.

Burning pastilles

Burning some kind of fumigatory
substance as an aid to health has been
practised all over the world for many
centuries, from joss sticks in India, China
and ten million student rooms, to the
acupuncturist's moxa cones. These
fragrant pastilles date from around 1910.

Pianist's finger stretcher

This seriously fearsome device was perfected in the USA around 1910 to help pianists with small hands improve their stretch, so they could hit the octave-and-a-few-as-well chords demanded by the likes of those radicals Stravinsky and Debussy. The composer Schumann is believed to have destroyed his hands using an earlier version, so be warned.

Toilet

The manufacturer of this 1870s water
closet was a plumber, Mr Jennings, who
had installed such WCs at the 1851 Great
Exhibition in London's Hyde Park. In public
toilets the cost of using a WC was a
penny, hence the saying 'to spend a
penny'. Mr Jennings's main competitor
was the better-known Thomas Crapper:
but for him we might be 'going for a Jen'
to this very day.

Light spectacles

For reading in the dark, these glasses with lights on were devised in the USA in the early 1930s. A brilliant idea, marred only by the problem for the wearer of having to lug a cell battery around to power them, and the danger of electrocution during a rainstorm.

Transport

'Everywhere is walking distance if you have the time'
Steven Wright

Anti-dazzler

The instructions are straightforward, but
it's hard to tell whether this German-
made thingy from the 1930s would
actually work or not. Apparently you
attach it to the pillar behind the driver's
head (by the door) and then angle it
to stop the dazzle from oncoming lights.
But wouldn't this restrict your vision
to an alarming extent?

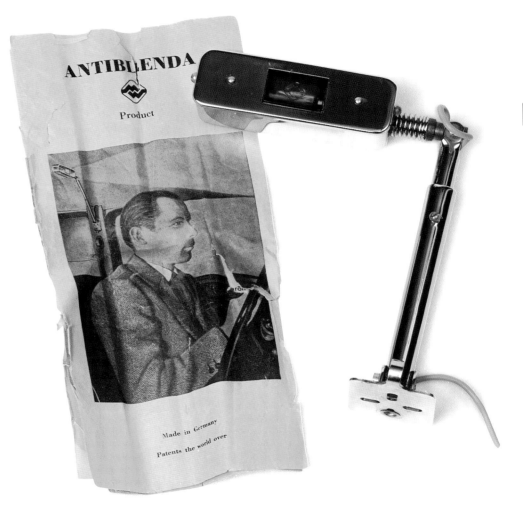

Car horn

The Lautovox, made in Lyon, France, in the early years of the 20th century, was activated by gases from the exhaust pipe, which was attached to the business end by a flexible tube. The car and the tube have long gone, but in the interests of research for this book, we blew hard into the horn. It's painfully loud.

Ball accelerometer

This cross between a roulette wheel
and a backgammon board was used in
the 1920s and 1930s to test the braking
power of vehicles: the balls were set in
position, and the brake efficiency was
worked out by checking the position of
the balls after the vehicle had stopped.
The spirit level is there to ensure that
the machine was set up properly.

Steering wheel heaters

Once auto electrics became reliable and
cars could be fitted with cigarette lighters
in the 1920s, all kinds of devices popped
up to take advantage of this invention.
One such is this pair of steering wheel
heaters: plug the end into the lighter
socket and tie the heaters to the wheel,
wait a while and then, hey presto!
Warmed and lightly singed wood for
those chilly mornings.

Car map holder

To save stopping when they needed
to consult a road map, motorists in the
1920s could use this car map holder.
The map was placed in the holder on the
top, and the curved part was positioned
on the driver's leg. The handle may
be elegant, but given its position, the
consequences of having to make an
emergency stop, or of a head-on collision,
are too frightful to contemplate.

Motorcyclist's pipe

Smoking a pipe was the epitome of
manliness in the mid-1920s, and this
ingenious little number meant that
motorcyclists could enjoy a puff or two
on the road; the mesh grille stopped the
wind from over-igniting or blowing out the
lit tobacco. It also solved the problem of
knocking out the hot ashes or dottle on
your handlebars at speed and having
them fly up your jacket sleeve.

Hand windscreen wiper

Drivers of open-top touring cars were the
boy racers of the 1920s. In wet weather
they clipped these handy portable wipers
over the windscreen and pushed the
handle to wipe away the rain – often
while changing gear with one hand and
steering with the other.

Coachman's belly warmer

To protect James from the worst of the
harsh late-Victorian winter weather, this
slightly convex belly warmer was filled
with hot water and fitted under his
coachman's coat. This probably helps
to account for his rotund appearance
in contemporary pictures.

Miscellaneous

'Everything that can be invented, has been invented.'
Charles H Duell

Sergeant-major's distance stick

A wonderful thing, military exactness:
when closed, this may look like a typical
World War I sergeant-major's swagger
stick but, open, it becomes the martinet's
bosom companion. It was used to
measure between lines of soldiers on
parade, to ensure that they were just so
far apart – and not one jot, tittle or iota
more or less.

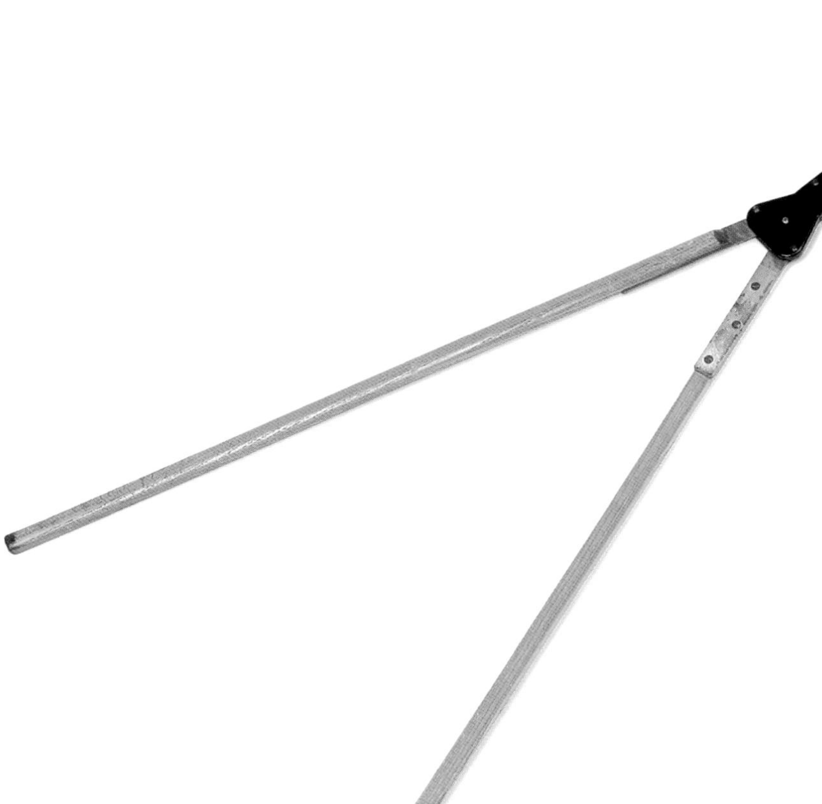

Spade pusher

To help the late-Victorian gardener or
outdoor worker push a spade into frozen
or hard ground, this spade pusher was tied
to the boot or shoe; the metal ridge at
the back fitted over the spade, enabling
pressure to be applied without hurting the
digger or ruining the footwear. Why isn't
this sort of thing around today?

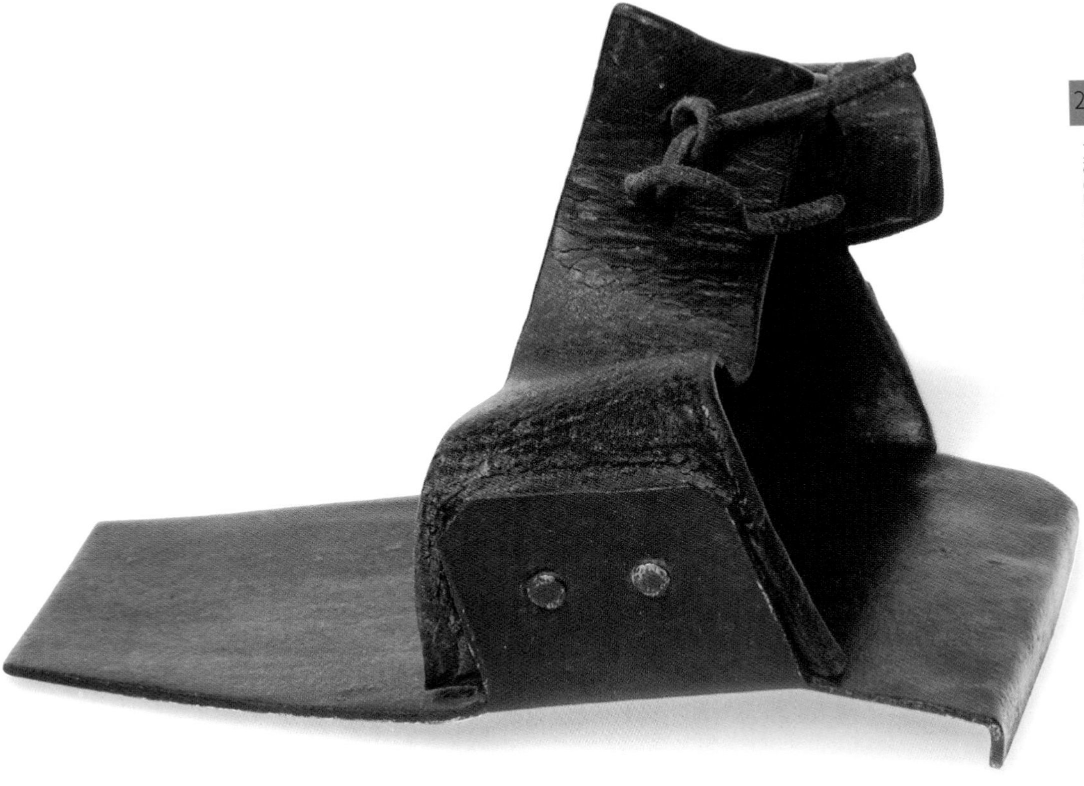

Police smelling salts

*'With a sigh of relief, Eveline fainted
dead away…'*
Victorian ladies made quite a career
of fainting, mainly due to tightly laced
corsets. Police constables therefore
carried smelling salts – made from
a strong solution of ammonia – in a
container about the size of a whistle,
to revive the ladies and prevent them
from cluttering up the Queen's highway
for any longer than was strictly necessary.

Rope maker

This early 20th-century winder could be
used equally for making rope, string or
wool yarn. Its descendants, often all but
identical, are still in use around the world.

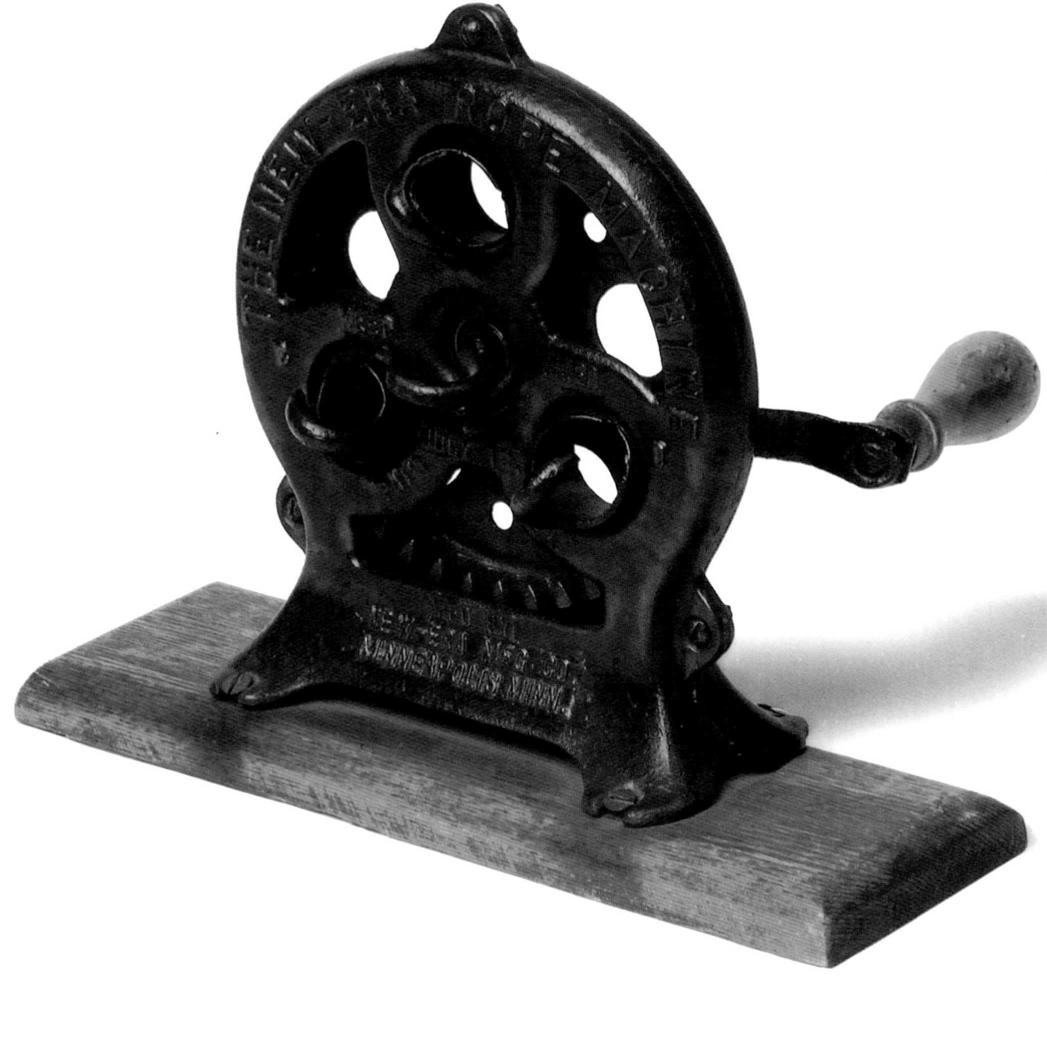

Music-hall clacker

People who made up music-hall audiences
worked hard to get the money to go
to the show, and they expected their
entertainment to come up to scratch.
These clackers were sold for a penny
outside Victorian halls, and made a terrible
noise when the handle was turned; any
performer subjected to this would know
that the act hadn't gone down well.

Person mover

This gruesome Victorian invention was put around the detainee's wrist and pulled tight, enabling the detainer to move his captive without trouble. However, both the detainer's hands were needed to keep the pressure constant, and if the detainee either used the undetained hand or had friends nearby, the efficacy of the device was reduced severely.

ACKNOWLEDGEMENTS

Thanks to George Taylor for the photography, and to Neil Baber,
Lewis Birchon and Ali Myer at David & Charles.

IK

All author's royalties from the sale of this book will be given to Kith and Kids, an innovative charity co-founded in 1969 by Maurice Collins OBE. The organization supports disabled children, adults and their families with practical help, offering a variety of projects and programmes, and attempts to influence UK policy makers in local authorities and government.

Each year Kith and Kids run a series of initiatives – three Social Development projects, a Friendship scheme, Advocacy and Summer programmes. Under the ethos of self-help, participating families can act as trustees and help with volunteer training and projects, but most importantly be part of a mutual support network. This principle of the founding families is still upheld 35 years on.

Radical thinker, innovator, business entrepreneur and charity fundraiser, Maurice Collins has been committed to improving the services and quality of life for people with a learning, physical or sensory disability for almost 40 years.

Contact Kith and Kids: telephone 020 8801 7432; visit the website **www.kithandkids.org.uk**